"The Bus Leaders Essential Guide to Innovation"

How to generate ground-breaking ideas and bring them to market

Stephen Dann

Published in the United Kingdom by Business Impact Solutions Ltd

Book design & layout by Velin@Perseus-Design.com

Email: bisbooks@businessimpactsolutions.co.uk
Website: www.businessimpactsolutions.co.uk

Paperback : 978-1-7399798-6-7

First Edition

The Business Leaders Essential Guide to Innovation

Innovation is so essential in business today and yet at the same time is so rarely properly applied or implemented.

Most businesses are founded on the back of a great idea, a true piece of innovation or a realisation that something could be done differently or better. But innovation is a sequence of ideas and actions that will take you forwards into the future, not a one-off event.

One of the prime reasons that businesses fail is because they run out of ideas or the energy to pursue them. They also often lack the discipline and process to put those ideas into practise.

In *The Business Leaders Essential Guide to Innovation*, renowned business adviser, Stephen Dann sets out the methods, the tools, and the techniques to enable your business to create ground-breaking ideas and implement them.

Whether you are a business owner, director, or entrepreneur, *The Business Leaders Essential Guide to Innovation* enables you to progress the right ideas with the greatest opportunity for your business, and to invest your time in developing new concepts and ideas that will give you a robust way forward.

You discover:

- How to generate new ideas
- How to select the best ideas
- How to develop and deliver innovation
- How to keep innovation projects on track
- The process to ensure your plans are implemented
- What's going to get in your way

Acknowledgements

Back in the late 1970's, as a student I picked up a second-hand copy of Edward de Bono's book "The 5-day Course in Thinking". Until then, I had thought that thinking was like breathing - it was just something you did. It had never occurred to me that you could learn to think, but I just filed it as "interesting". 20 years later I was on a flight and there in the inflight business magazine was a feature about de Bono's Six Thinking Hats®* which suddenly provided practical application, tools, and techniques which we could use to tackle real business issues.

There are so many people who have inspired my long-term fascination with innovation, and I have drawn extensively on their ideas and techniques in developing the approach outlined in this book. In acknowledging their contribution, I apologise that I cannot identify and thank everyone individually.

However specific thanks should go to:

* Six Thinking Hats is a registered trademark of de Bono Ltd used with permission from www.debono.com where more information on Edward de Bono can be found.

Edward de Bono whose tools, techniques and thinking have deeply influenced my approach and set me on a lifelong path of creativity and innovation.

Caspar de Bono for his helpful comments, guidance, and interest in this project.

Chuck Dymer for writing the foreword and for first showing me that the work of de Bono had practical application in business.

Robert Fisher and the team at Indigo Business Services who have consistently delivered outstanding training to support innovation projects and implementing creative change agendas.

This stuff only works when it gets off the page and into practice, so the many clients who have trusted me to help them develop innovative products and cultures.

In particular those brave individuals who have continued to think differently, find fresh solutions and new paradigms, often in the face of great resistance - you know who you are.

Foreword

Stephen Dann and I first met at a Six Thinking Hats workshop in central London. I was the presenter and Stephen a participant—a star participant. He asked probing and insightful questions. He participated in and often led small group discussions. He shared interesting and relevant examples of what was working and not working in his business.

Stephen left the Six Thinking Hats workshop with a lot of ideas. But as you'll quickly realize when you read this book, Stephen knows ideas have little value until applied. He makes that point in the very first sentence of his introduction.

Not long after that workshop concluded, Stephen, phoned and asked if I would visit him at his office. He wanted to discuss how his team could be introduced to and make practical use of The Six Thinking Hats. You will learn more about the Six Thinking Hats and how you can put them to work in Part One of the book.

His office was stunning with large windows that provided views of the grounds while inviting rich sunlight into the space. With such bright light it was easy to view the furnishings as well as the pictures and information that hung on the walls. One of the wall hangings I couldn't help but notice was the Vision Statement.

Many businesses feel compelled to craft a vision statement. Wikipedia defines a vision statement as "...an inspirational statement of an idealistic emotional future of a company or group." So, most of those businesses write lofty and meaningless phrases, call it their vision statement and file them away.

But the vision statement Stephen crafted was not like that at all. I was utterly astounded by his vision statement and asked Stephen if I could have a copy. That vision statement appears below.

This vision statement is in Mind Map format, a diagram that visually organizes the information. The central concept of the Mind Map is **Our Vision**, and ten branches elucidate that central concept. Each branch consists of an emoji-like image and a simple directive. For example, the third branch (moving clockwise) has an image of three people gathered around a meeting table. The directive is "Stay small enough to give personal service."

Here's what amazed me. I could not only read and then imagine the vision, but I could also SEE it. According to my dictionary, the word "vision" is not limited to the anticipation of what may come to be—some ideal future state. "Vision" is primarily defined as the act of sensing with the eyes. Stephen broke the boundaries of most vision statements which use words to describe a future state. His vision statement consisted of words and images that described what the company could do to differentiate itself now and in the future. Instead of being "pie in the sky," it was grounded.

Stephen saw the value of a vision statement in how it could be implemented and not merely thought about. To him the statement was practical as well as inspirational. As he writes in the section about Where do I look for ideas?: "To create genuinely new approaches, it is inevitable that existing practices, policies, and products should be scrutinized and challenged rigorously."

To reiterate the content and value of this book: "Creativity is defined as having new ideas. Innovation is about putting those ideas into practice with commercial impact. *So, you will need the tools for both thinking and doing"* (italics mine).

The Business Leaders Essential Guide to Innovation provides you with practical tools to generate new ideas, select the best of those ideas, and then develop them into products and services that will provide your business with commercial advantage. It was these very tools that enabled Stephen to develop the novel and highly effective vision statement.

My only criticism of this book is that it was not available 30 years ago. It was then, in the early days of my consultancy, that I facilitated a creative thinking session for a client that manufactured denim clothing—jeans, jackets, etc. I guided the attendees of that creative session to produce, in less than 6 hours, more than 850 ideas. I took their ideas, which were on Post-It Notes, back to my office and transcribed them to Word format. I then printed each idea on a post-card size document. The end result was a uniform deck of 850 idea cards that the client could sort and deal with as they would like.

Trouble was, they did not know how to meaningfully sort the ideas, or refine them, or set up development plans. When I visited the client a few weeks after the event, the card deck of ideas remained on the client's desk exactly where I placed it. I thought the creative session was a triumph; the client thought it a waste of time.

Had I had Stephen's book then, both the client and I would have known precisely what to do with those ideas. As you will read:

"Simply asking people just to come up with ideas or suggestions is unlikely to yield ground-breaking results." I can certainly verify that!

In addition to tools that help you target the best areas for idea generation and tools to help generate ideas, you'll receive tools to winnow the ideas to those worthy of development. And then you'll receive the tools needed to rapidly develop, scale, and test those ideas.

The Business Leaders Essential Guide to Innovation is a gem of a book.

John George Kemeny, computer scientist, developer of Basic programming language, and former President of Dartmouth College, said: "It is the greatest achievement of a teacher to enable his students to surpass him." I thank Stephen Dann for my great achievement as a Six Thinking Hats presenter.

Chuck Dymer
Founder and president of Brilliance Activator, a creative thinking and innovation consultancy. He is proud to be the first Six Thinking Hats Lifetime Master Trainer Emeritus.

Introduction

I have never really understood why it is that innovation can be cool, fashionable, and so essential in business and at the same time be so rarely properly applied or implemented.

I would imagine that you founded your business on the back of a great idea, a true piece of innovation or a realisation you could do something differently or better. From that germ of an idea, you built and developed it to its present condition. If you have read the first book in this series, which focuses on business growth, you will have already identified your key issues and set out action plans.

But where do you go next?

Innovation is not a one-off event. It is a sequence of ideas and actions that will take you forwards into the future. Your competitors will not have stood still. They will have observed your innovation and will be doing all they can to copy and to improve on what you have achieved so far.

One of the prime reasons that businesses fail is because they run out of ideas or the energy to pursue them. They also often lack the discipline to put those ideas into practise.

Creativity is defined as the having new ideas. Innovation is about putting those ideas into practise with a commercial impact. So, you will need the tools for both thinking **and** doing.

So, if you have too many ideas and are lacking the disciplines to implement them properly, or have too few ideas, or maybe even none at all, then this book is here to give you a guide. This ensures you progress the right ideas with the greatest opportunity for your business, and you invest your time in developing new concepts and ideas that will give you a robust way forward.

Table of Contents

1.

The Innovation Journey

We need to draw the distinction between creativity and innovation. They are not the same thing.

Creativity is all about having new ideas and new concepts, innovation is all about turning those ideas into reality, so they deliver commercial impact.

But what sort of ideas?

It is tempting to think of innovation purely in the sense of new products and services, or new technologies, but innovation can be and should be applied to every single part of the business model.

Some of the most innovative companies in the world do not actually have the most innovative products. In many cases they were not the first in the field either but have chosen other areas of innovation to excel in to achieve competitive and commercial advantage.

There are 3 key phases in the journey which we will explore:

1. How to generate new ideas

New ideas do not happen by accident. They are created through a deliberate creative process which is both focused and purposeful. The focus should be firmly set on opportunities and challenges with clear goals. Building a substantial list of concepts and ideas takes far more than just the odd brainstorming session. It is essential in this creative phase to avoid all judgement or assessment of ideas to allow the creative side of your brain to work effectively. Every one of us has a creative side to our brain, so idea generation should not be restricted just to "creative" people.

2. How to select the best ideas

Once a substantial pool of potential concepts and ideas are established the next stage is to narrow down the focus so that only the best opportunities are progressed. An idea rejected in this phase does not mean it is a bad idea; it may lack detail, understanding or be too conceptual to enable it to progress. Rejected ideas are valuable trigger points for further ideas so are worth filing for future reference. Sometimes the selection process becomes tainted with teams erring on what they feel are safe and acceptable options rather than their more creative ideas. Either way it is crucial to select a limited number of options to take forward for early-stage testing followed by further research and potential development.

3. How to develop and deliver innovation

Turning ideas into reality is the toughest part of the innovation journey. True innovators often find the pace, detail, and practical barriers frustrating and feel the inspiration and energy draining away. Too often they will then just generate further new ideas. This effectively disrupts the team who are wrestling with implementing the previous one. Turning creative ideas into reality requires clear disciplined project management. This is a completely different mindset to the idea generation phase. Beyond this, growing and scaling is a significant challenge which was covered in the first book in this series (The Business Leaders Essential Guide to Growth).

How to use this book

If you are searching for new ideas – start in section 1.

If you already have loads of ideas listed already, you can skip section 1 and focus on how to select the best ones in section 2.

If you are struggling to develop and implement, then section 3 will put you on track.

If you find innovation as fascinating as I do, then check out the Recommended Reading at the end.

If you want to ramp up growth and scale your innovation, then check out the first book in this series.

HOW TO GENERATE NEW IDEAS

In this stage, the key areas where new thinking is required are identified and new ideas generated.

2.

What's the overall process?

To start we need to set out the Thinking Agenda.

Simply asking people just to come up with ideas or suggestions is unlikely to yield ground-breaking results. Because the ideas are inevitably poor, they are not progressed, the team becomes discouraged and therefore they cease to contribute. Right at the start it is important not to assume that everyone understands the innovation process or that they are comfortable with it. Innovation is challenging, hard work, exhausting, and frustrating; but ultimately extremely satisfying and rewarding.

However, remember that innovation and change go hand in hand - for most people change creates uncertainty and is threatening.

Those of us who relish it are a minority. So, having a clearly defined process and taking the time to train and brief your team fully will be essential to successful innovation. Time invested up front in this process with the team will pay dividends later.

The Four Key Stages

The ideation process progresses through 4 stages, each requiring a different set of tools and a different mindset.

1. Targeting
Confirm and clarify the Objectives and Focus

2. Expanding
Open up the thinking to generate a high volume of ideas

3. Contracting
Narrow down the thinking onto the best ideas

4. Actioning
Schedule and manage activity to rapidly develop and scale

We will cover the first 2 stages in this section.

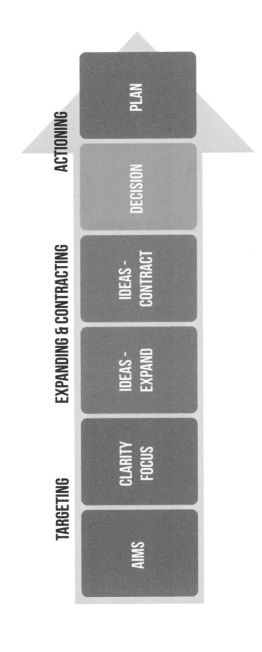

THINKING AGENDA

TARGETING

EXPANDING & CONTRACTING

ACTIONING

AIMS

CLARITY FOCUS

IDEAS - EXPAND

IDEAS - CONTRACT

DECISION

PLAN

Without a clear purpose it is easy to generate lots of wild ideas, lose focus, and fail to move the business forwards fast enough. To start with we need to have a clear focus, this needs to be regularly restated to avoid drifting off into creative side-lines.

Aims, Goals and Objectives
So, what is your overall objective?
Why are you doing this?
It could be that your current offering is being hurt by a competitor or a new customer need has emerged, or a new technology is now available.

The aim, the goal or objective will provide a constant reference point to ensure that the innovation process is kept focussed and on track. It's a good idea to set sub objectives also which define more specific achievable steps or stages. Any objectives which require urgent action right now should also be noted. As always these should be quantified so that progress can be measured and have specific target dates for completion.

Focus
Having set some goals, we now need to clarify the focus for innovation without being too prescriptive. It is essential to have some boundaries so that the process does not become clogged up with worthy but irrelevant ideas. Speed is crucial, so a more specific focus will enable faster outcomes.

For example:

Are we aiming to develop ideas for existing users who we already know and understand, or new ones where our knowledge may be more limited?

What is the scale of the goal for the offering? Are we seeking to make small incremental improvements, steady evolution, or disrupt the market?

3.

Where do I look for ideas?

In the build up towards formal idea generation activities it is useful to develop broader areas of thinking in advance. This can help identify specific areas to concentrate on, provide direct stimulation to the thought process, and allow people to think more expansively and imaginatively.

To create genuinely new approaches, it is inevitable that existing practises, policies, and products should be scrutinised and challenged rigorously. There can often be resistance to this as people may have spent many years building their careers on what currently exists. However, holding on to the past is not a good way to design the future - in the same way that it is not a good idea to drive a car solely using the rear-view mirrors. The lessons of the past may provide some useful insight, but that experience exists in a different context to the one we are faced with today and tomorrow. The future is like a different country - they speak a different language there.

Market Sector and Customer behaviour

Probably the first place to consider is the market. Markets are dynamic, changing and evolving all the time. Businesses often create a level of perceived wisdom about the way their market or customers act and behave. Often that wisdom is based on old established thinking from many years ago which gradually morphs into a traditional embedded mindset on "the way things work". Sometimes established customer segmentation or personas exist largely in the mind of the marketer rather than the reality of the market. It is safe to start by assuming that perceived wisdom on markets and customers is usually wrong until you can prove it otherwise. So:

- What is happening in your market?
- How is it evolving and changing?
- What new challenges behaviours and problems are emerging?
- How are decision makers changing?
- What new issues might they be facing?
- How is the structure of the market changing?
- How are peoples buying habits changing?
- What facets of the past will no longer be true in the future?

- How will people respond to new technology?
- What experiences and behaviours in everyday life will people transfer to business decisions?

Problems to be solved

Customers are ultimately seeking to find a solution to a problem which may either be a specific need or a more emotional want. They will be seeking either to avoid a pain point which hurts them or places them at risk or to secure some form of gain which enhances their status or gives pleasure. People generally seek to move away from pain and towards gain.

So, what are the key pain points that your customers feel today or are likely to feel in the future? These are key needs that will have to be satisfied by any product or service that you offer.

What might your customers be looking for from a gain perspective? These will be the key wants that will drive the underlying emotion behind all purchase decisions.

Enhancement or Adaptation

Innovation does not necessarily mean a total fresh start. There are many situations where simply enhancing or adapting existing products or services can have a radical impact. Customers often take the established functionality of a product for granted and make their decisions on the extras, the enhancements and even the packaging.

Innovation

There are broadly three types of innovation: developing efficiency, sustaining, and transforming. These carry different levels of risk and potential impact.

The simplest and most common is focused on developing efficiency - enhancing and improving existing practises and products without fundamentally changing the business model or the product itself.

More risky and impactful is innovation focused on sustaining the existing business model often through developing new products and services targeted at existing markets and customer segments.

Finally, transformational innovation seeks to radically change or disrupt the market, usually taking the business well outside the arena of its traditional experience and competency. Clearly at the start of any innovation process it is important to understand the scale of ambition before generating ideas.

Competitor

Many innovation initiatives are triggered by competitive activity. Maybe a competitor has launched a new product which is now taking market share away from you. Customers may be being swayed by the newest and latest rather than your established tried and tested offering. As we shall see, there are some dangers in seeking to emulate competitors, but their activities can also provide a useful impetus for new ideas.

It is worth establishing the strengths and weaknesses of your competitors' offerings from a customer as well as a technical perspective. Then consider the following:

- Could you do more for less?
  Is there any way in which you could deliver higher quality, better service, or more features at lower cost?
- Could you do less for more?
  In many cases a stripped back version of a product which performs the core task extremely well can demand a price premium.
- Now ignore the product.
  Let's assume your product is identical to the one produced by your competitor in every respect including the price. What are the other components that surround the product that would be good targets for innovative thinking? for example:
  Service?
  Packaging?
  Niche focus?

Sector?

Processes?

The Curse of the Red Queen

The risk of focusing too much on what competitors are doing and trying to emulate them is that you will always be one step behind. Because the new product they have just launched which is hurting you will be superseded by the next new product they are working on which you do not yet know about. Therefore, if you simply match what they have already launched, you will then be caught off guard by what they launch next. It is crucial therefore to leapfrog their latest product to get ahead of the game. In "Alice in Wonderland", when Alice played chess with the Red Queen, the Red Queen changed the rules after every move. The rules do not stay the same, they change constantly.

Design Criteria

When developing initial ideas, it is useful to set out the core design criteria which define the boundaries on what the product must have, should have, could have, and won't have.

Must
    Essential. Must-haves & non-negotiables.
Should
    Important. Should-haves & important features

Could
Optional. Could-haves & optional features
Wont
No way. Won't-haves, things that are definitely not on the table. Non-negotiables

Target Hit List

Thinking about innovation is not a one-off event. It is often beneficial to have an established clear list of areas which require innovative thinking. By publicising these and making them visible for everyone in the team to see it enables the entire business to be engaged in ideas and suggestions. It is helpful to provide a focus framework to define the specific issues, challenges, or opportunities for ideas:

Focus on Improvement
 – what improvements are we trying to make?

Focus on Problems
 – what problems are we trying to solve?

Focus on New Ideas
 - where do we want new ideas?

The stronger the focus and the better the guidance provided to innovation teams, the more likely they are to generate a substantial volume of high-quality ideas. As in so many aspects of business, the quality of the brief has a direct impact on the quality and scale of the outcome. So, in your enthusiasm to dive into the creative process please do not skimp on defining the brief and energising the team.

4.

How do I generate new ideas?

So now you have clarity of focus and an understanding of where you are going to look for ideas, we will explore a range of techniques to generate new ideas. This is by no means a definitive list of methods and approaches for ideation, but every one of these has been deployed in practice, generating thousands of new ideas. The aim in ideation is to generate as many ideas as possible so that there is a rich and varied pool to assess.

Jettison - Existing ideas and Yesterday's thinking

One of the most common barriers to generating new ideas is the battery of old ideas which have been thought of before and either not progressed, been rejected, or failed. Brainstorming sessions are doomed to failure if all they do is regurgitate and recycle past thinking. Sometimes when teams participate in brainstorming, they are unable to embrace new thinking until they have shared ideas that they have been thinking about already. So, the key first step is to purge yesterday's thinking to free up minds for genuine innovation. When you start a brainstorming session ask everyone for their initial ideas, establish the current situation and the current thinking. Then list the suggested alternatives that have already been produced. These will be the obvious ideas, the old ideas, the pet projects, and anything else which is at the front of people's minds. Capture all of these and then start again. You may wish to come back to yesterday's thinking as a trigger for new ideas and concepts in due course. (Tip: if you are feeling bold, tear the pages off the flip charts and dump them!) You will now have cleansed minds to enable them to create genuinely new ideas.

Brainstorming Process

The rules of brainstorming are remarkably simple. They are designed to ensure that you use the specific part of the brain for creating ideas and allow those ideas to flow freely. So, no idea should be judged, qualified, or discussed. Quantity of ideas is essential, not quality. Crazy ideas are completely welcome and building on each other's ideas whilst brainstorming is good. What may seem to be a wildly impossible idea may trigger a different train of thought by someone else which leads to viable innovation. Ensure all ideas are captured. All you need is a wall and lots of "post it" notes.

Solo Thinking

Brainstorming is generally considered to be a group activity, however there is a risk of thinking coalescing around the group so that more extreme ideas are not put forward. "Group think" is an enemy of new thinking and innovation. Therefore, I favour initial thinking on an individual basis so that the full breadth of ideas is brought to the table and everyone's voice is equal. So, for individual thinking, use "post It" notes, write one idea (neatly) per "post It" note, present your notes back to the team and stick the "post it" note on the wall. So, you will now have a wide selection of initial ideas. Avoid the temptation to start developing them or judging them yet – that time will come, but for now you need to keep generating ideas.

Trigger Questions

Now let's apply a range of different perspectives using challenging questions to provoke triggers for innovation:

- What would we do if we were a new start-up company?
- What would we do if we had unlimited access to money and resources?
- What would we do if we had no resources at all?
- What would Google or Apple do if we were taken over by them?
- What would we do if our 'way of working' would be forbidden by law?

- What would my favourite comic/movie hero from my childhood do?
- What would my competitor need to do to destroy me?
- What is holding you back from substantial growth?
- What would have to happen to grow by 10x?
- Where are you weakest or most vulnerable?

Next, we will use some techniques based on the ground-breaking work of Edward De Bono, the originator of "Lateral Thinking".

Concept Extraction - expanding the idea pool

One of the most fruitful ways to expand the pool of ideas is to use the ones you have already generated as a trigger point for further creativity.

Firstly, we must distinguish between concepts and ideas.
Some of the initial suggestions will be specific and actionable ideas.
Others will be much broader concepts.

An **idea** – is anything which could be taken away and actioned.
A **concept** – is broader, less specific and you cannot action it.

So, taking each suggestion proposed so far, decide if it is a concept or an idea.

a) If it is an idea, find the concept behind it, then propose further ideas.

Consider what the broader concept is behind that idea.

Pose the question; "the idea is a way of …...?" to establish what the underlying concept is. Then think of 2 other specific ideas which would deliver on it.

b) If it is a concept, propose 2 more ideas to fulfil it.

Consider other ways to deliver the concept.

Pose the question "How else can we ….?".

Then think of 2 additional ideas to deliver on it.

By extracting the concept behind each idea, we can rapidly multiply the number of ideas. This can be repeated several times over until no new concepts or ideas emerge. Some of these ideas may be similar or identical but arrived at from different perspectives.

CONCEPT EXTRACTION

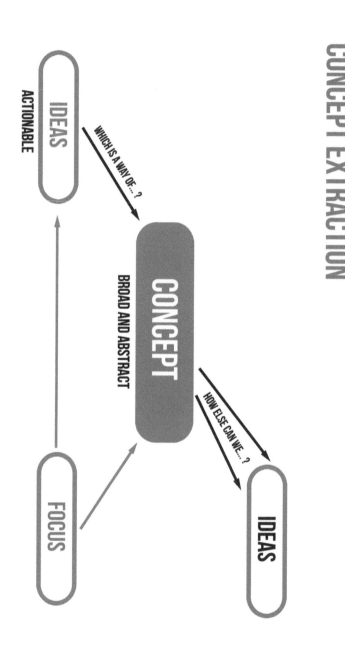

- Sort suggestions by Concept or Actionable idea
- For each Concept generate 2 ideas
- For each Idea, generate the Concept and 2 more ideas

CONCEPT EXTRACTION EXAMPLE 1

IDEAS	CONCEPTS	ALTERNATIVE IDEAS

An Example: Focus: How to make the company adopt sustainability

In this example the team has been tasked to generate ideas on how the company might improve its approach to sustainability. We will use just 4 of the suggestions from the brainstorm:

- Convince the CEO
- Influence New Product Development process
- Create Education & Fun packs for staff children
- Sustainability displays in offices

The first 2 are Concepts (broad) and the second 2 are Ideas (actionable)

CONCEPT EXTRACTION EXAMPLE 2

IDEAS	CONCEPTS	ALTERNATIVE IDEAS
	CONVINCE THE CEO	
	INFLUENCE NEW PRODUCT DEVELOPMENT PROCESS	
CREATE EDUCATION & FUN PACKS FOR STAFF CHILDREN		
SUSTAINABILITY DISPLAYS IN OFFICES		

So, starting with the **Concepts**:

What ideas could there be on "How can we convince the CEO?"

Idea suggestions included: developing the business case and influence his family (his children were learning about sustainability at school).

How could we "influence the NPD process"; Ideas: build sustainability into product specifications from day 1 and launch in-company sustainability award.

Now looking at the actionable ideas:

"Create Education & fun packs for staff children" is a way of doing what?
The concept behind this idea is "improve staff commitment".
How else might we do that?
Idea: Set up a volunteer / sabbatical programme.

"Sustainability displays in offices" is a way of doing what?
The concept behind this idea is: "Show the company commitment".
How else might we do that?
Idea: "Sponsor a university programme or professor".

CONCEPT EXTRACTION EXAMPLE 3

IDEAS	CONCEPTS	ALTERNATIVE IDEAS
DEVELOP THE BUSINESS CASE	CONVINCE THE CEO	INFLUENCE HIS FAMILY
MAKE SUSTAINABILITY PART OF THE SPECIFICATION	INFLUENCE NEW PRODUCT DEVELOPMENT PROCESS	COMPANY SUSTAIN AWARD
CREATE EDUCATION & FUN PACKS FOR STAFF CHILDREN	IMPROVE STAFF COMMITMENT	VOLUNTEER / SABBATICAL PROGRAMME
SUSTAINABILITY DISPLAYS IN OFFICES	SHOW COMPANY COMMITMENT	SPONSOR A UNIVERSITY PROFESSOR

So, by extracting concepts and driving further ideas we have extended the idea pool and opened up new thinking.

But we are not done yet.

Random Word

One of the other techniques pioneered by Edward de Bono enables you to borrow attributes from completely unrelated items and apply them to your challenge.

Using the random word technique, you select a noun at random and define at least 5 of its key attributes. (Tip: Avoid listing too many attributes)

Then consider how those attributes might apply to your focus and generate ideas arising from them.

RANDOM WORD

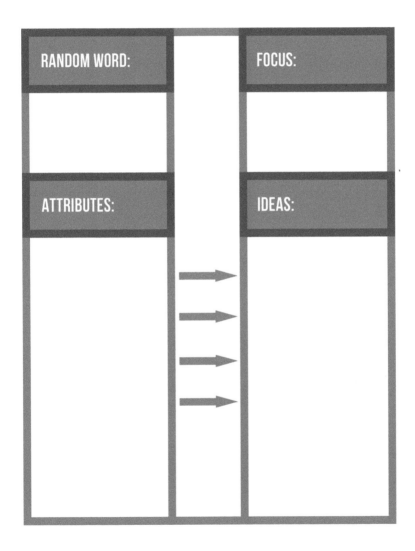

RANDOM WORD:

FOCUS:

ATTRIBUTES:

IDEAS:

- Select a noun at random.
- Define its attributes
- Apply them to the focus
- Generate new ideas

To find a random word, pick up any book (or magazine).

Think of a number not greater than the total number of pages of the book and open the book on that page.

Think of another number (not greater than the number of lines on the page) and count down to select a line on the page, then pick the first noun on that line as your random word.

So, let's go back to the previous example of the team tasked to generate ideas on how the company might improve its approach to sustainability.

We have found our Random Word which is: **"Dog"**

There is no obvious connection between a dog and a company searching for ways to improve sustainability.

Start by listing some attributes of a dog:

four legs
loyal
best friend
lives for 10 years

work or pet
tail
bark

Then apply each of these attributes to our focus to improve sustainability.

What ideas come from "four legs"?

- 4 legs make a dog stable – so we need to have a stable programme, maybe it should have 4 "legs" too.
- 4 legs enable a dog to run, walk, jump and be agile, flexible, fast, and adaptable – how does agility and adaptability apply to our sustainability approach.
- If a dog loses a leg, it can still run and live a full life – so if one part of our programme doesn't work out then it's OK so long as the other 3 do.

Then continue with each of the attributes:

RANDOM WORD

RANDOM WORD:

DOG

FOCUS:

HOW TO MAKE THE COMPANY ADOPT SUSTAINABILITY

ATTRIBUTES:

IDEAS:

ATTRIBUTES	IDEAS
FOUR LEGS	INCREASE BUSINESS STABILITY 4 LEGS OF SUSTAINABILITY
LOYAL	INCREASE STAFF & CUSTOMER LOYALTY
BEST FRIEND	DEVELOP 2-WAY RELATIONSHIPS BE THE NO1, BEST RELATIONSHIP
LIVES 10 YEARS	NOT A ONE OFF - LIFECYCLE, THEN START AGAIN. START THE NEXT INITIATIVE BEFORE THIS ONE ENDS
WORK OR PET	COMMERCIAL V EMOTIONAL FACTORS
TAIL	COMMUNICATION IS ESSENTIAL HAPPY CUSTOMERS / TEAM
BARK	ALERTS TO AVOID FAILURE / ANNOUNCE SUCCESS

Now go back and expand the idea pool further by extracting concepts and ideas from each of these.

There is no limit to how many times the random word exercise can be used – just keep going to generate more ideas.

You should now have a substantial list of ideas.

Initial Shortlist Vote

It is useful to get an initial view from the team generating the ideas on which ones they think have the most merit, even at this early stage.

So, ask the team to vote on their favoured ideas.

Depending on the number of ideas in the pool, allow 3 or 4 votes each.

Avoid defining the basis for these votes and leave participants free to vote for whichever they find the most:
Interesting
Powerful
Practical
Impactful

From this it will become clear where the focus and energy of thinking is strongest. Depending on your goals, this may mean that you are ready to move on to the next stage or should go back and try harder.

Sometimes teams will naturally vote for ideas which they believe will be acceptable to management. This will simply reinforce existing practices rather than be a trigger for genuine innovation and new paradigms. So, if you feel that everyone is playing it safe, go back and start again!

Six Thinking Hats ®

One of the most widely used of Edward de Bono's tools, is Six Thinking Hats®. This can be used in many contexts to improve the quality of thinking and decision making. Here we will use Six Thinking Hats® to help refine the opportunity and your thinking.

Six Hats can be used individually, or in a group, to ensure that the ideas and opportunities are thought through "in the round". Each of the hats represents a different mode of thinking, and by using each in turn its possible to rapidly gain a full and balanced perspective on a topic. The different modes of thinking (hats) are explored to drive the direction of future thinking with everyone using the same hat at the same time. Please note that each of the six hats is **not** a description of personal or personality style preferences.

SIX THINKING HATS®

THE SIX THINKING HATS	
BLUE HAT: THE CONDUCTOR'S HAT	**THINKING ABOUT AND MANAGING THE THINKING PROCESS** THE BLUE HAT IS THE CONTROL HAT. IT IS USED FOR THINKING ABOUT THINKING. THE BLUE HAT SETS THE AGENDA, FOCUS AND SEQUENCE, ENSURES THE GUIDELINES ARE OBSERVED AND ASKS FOR SUMMARIES, CONCLUSIONS, DECISIONS AND PLANS OF ACTION.
GREEN HAT: THE CREATIVE HAT	**GENERATING IDEAS** THE GREEN HAT IS FOR CREATIVE THINKING AND GENERATING NEW IDEAS, ALTERNATIVES, POSSIBILITIES AND NEW CONCEPTS.
RED HAT: THE HAT FOR THE HEART	**INTUITION AND FEELINGS** THE RED HAT IS ABOUT FEELINGS, INTUITIONS AND INSTINCTS. THE RED HAT INVITES FEELINGS WITHOUT JUSTIFICATION.
YELLOW HAT: THE OPTIMIST'S HAT	**BENEFITS AND VALUES** THE YELLOW HAT IS FOR A POSITIVE VIEW OF THINGS. IT LOOKS FOR THE BENEFITS AND VALUES.
BLACK HAT: THE JUDGE'S HAT	**CAUTION** THE BLACK HAT IDENTIFIES RISK. IT IS USED FOR CRITICAL JUDGEMENT AND MUST GIVE THE LOGICAL REASONS FOR CONCERNS. IT IS ONE OF THE MOST POWERFUL HATS.
WHITE HAT: THE FACTUAL HAT	**INFORMATION** THE WHITE HAT IS ALL ABOUT INFORMATION.WHAT INFORMATION YOU HAVE WHAT INFORMATION YOU NEED AND WHERE TO GET IT.

IMPORTANT POINTS TO NOTE

- THE HATS CAN BE USED ON YOUR OWN OR IN A GROUP
- IN GROUP DISCUSSIONS, IT IS ESSENTIAL THAT EVERYONE USES THE SAME HAT (STYLE OF THINKING) AT THE SAME TIME. THIS IS TO AVOID PERSONAL PREFERENCES AND CONFLICTS BETWEEN STYLES OF THINKING.
- THE BLACK HAT IS ESSENTIAL. IT IS A NECESSARY PART OF THE THINKING BUT IS OFTEN OVERUSED.
- TRAINING IN THE USE OF HATS INCLUDES HOW TO STRUCTURE THE HATS INTO SEQUENCES TO ADDRESS DIFFERENT SITUATIONS.

© COPYRIGHT EDWARD DE BONO LTD, TRADING AS DE BONO

* Six Thinking Hats is a registered trademark of de Bono Ltd used with permission from www.debono.com where more information on Edward de Bono can be found.

As with all creative thinking, time pressure is essential to keep the brain moving and energy level up. So, for this exercise, only allow a few minutes on each hat.

The six thinking modes fall into pairs:

Reality – subjective v objective
Red Hat: What's your gut feel about this idea? Do you love it or hate it?

White Hat: What facts do we have on this? What are the critical gaps in knowledge?

Assessment – benefits v risks
Yellow Hat: Why is this a great idea? What are the benefits

Black Hat: Why is this a bad idea? What are the difficulties, risks, and problems?

Design – creativity v planning
Green Hat: are there alternatives or further ideas? How do we overcome the (black hat) difficulties, risks, and problems?

Blue Hat: What are the next steps?

So, for each of the most voted for ideas run through the following sequence of hats:

Blue
Confirm the topic, agenda, and time allocation

Red
Gut feel, emotional reaction to the idea

White
Facts known and missing

Yellow
Positive views

Black
Negative views

Green
Alternatives and solutions to negatives

Blue
Next steps to develop the idea

SIX THINKING HATS® WORKSHEET

HAT	TIME	NOTES
BLUE HAT:		
RED HAT:		
WHITE HAT:		
YELLOW HAT:		
BLACK HAT:		
GREEN HAT:		
BLUE HAT:		

There should now be a more rounded view of these ideas – and you have probably generated a few more. These further ideas should be treated in the same way.

It is important but that any ideation process reaches a point of conclusion by the team who created the ideas so that they feel that all their ideas have been captured and extended wherever possible.

Now that we have completed the creative part of the process it will be time to move on and assess these ideas critically and rigorously to ensure that the best opportunities are progressed. This is a different mindset to the idea generation phase and therefore should not be attempted in the same session.

HOW TO SELECT
THE BEST IDEAS

In this stage, the pool of ideas is filtered and narrowed down to a manageable number of opportunities which have the greatest commercial viability.

5.

How do I decide which ideas to focus on?

If you have used all the tools and techniques explored in the previous section, you should now have a significant pool of ideas. It is not unusual to be faced with several hundred ideas. Every one of these has merit and potential and therefore the next stage in the journey is to evaluate and sort these to ensure that your development processes and business are not overwhelmed by too many initiatives. It is far preferable to take a very few ideas rapidly to fulfilment and then return to your idea pool for more, rather than attempt to progress too many too slowly and most likely fail.

Idea Pool Re-evaluation

So review and sort all ideas generated, not just those voted on in the ideation process (Though they should have special attention since the ideation team rated them highly).The following approaches will help narrow down the idea pool considerably:

- Clustering - form groups of similar or compatible ideas. It should not be surprising that similar ideas may emerge and therefore these can be clustered or drawn together.

- File those which are too creative for later consideration Some ideas are just too extreme and too creative. Whilst it is tempting to reject them, they should be retained for future reference. These may well prove to be a rich resource for genuinely bold innovation. I have often found that keeping at least one crazy wild idea in the mix is beneficial, if nothing else, it provides contrast to the safer, may be, lower impact solutions.

- Consider the balance between short, medium, and longer-term projects to ensure a balanced innovation pipeline.

- Select the revised "long" list
  You should now be able to trim back the idea pool for further assessment, but we have further to go to arrive at a shortlist.

Idea Matrix

There are many potential options to assess ideas on a matrix. It is very much a case of individual preference and circumstance on what the criteria should be. However, I favour using multiple criteria to ensure that the assessment captures the different priorities and dimensions of the business.

Firstly, let's consider each of the ideas in terms of their revenue potential and their feasibility or cost of development. Place the ideas on the matrix:

IDEA MATRIX

	REVENUE	
	HIGH/ FAVOURABLE	LOW / UNFAVOURABLE
FEASIBILITY / COST		
HIGH/ FAVOURABLE		

Clearly any idea which has high potential revenue and low cost of development should be retained in the process. By contrast anything with low revenue and high development cost should be eliminated.

Other potential axes for assessment could be:

Time to implement v market impact

Investment required v ease of copying by competitors

Impact on the business v difficulty to develop

Production cost v speed to market

Select the most favourable opportunities to proceed to your short list.

Opportunity Scorecard

So, we now need to apply greater levels of rigour to each of the shortlist ideas. In this stage we will develop a clear understanding of each opportunity with an objective assessment which explains the idea further and scores it. As a result, different ideas can be ranked alongside each other.

OPPORTUNITY SCORECARD

DESCRIPTION OF THE IDEA

PURPOSE - WHY ARE YOU DOING THIS, WHAT DO YOU WANT TO ACHIEVE?

HOW IMPORTANT IS IT, WHAT DIFFERENCE WILL IT MAKE?

WHAT IS THE DESIRED OUTCOME WHEN COMPLETED?

WHAT ARE THE SUCCESS CRITERIA?

WHAT IS THE BEST OUTCOME IF YOU GO AHEAD?

WHAT WILL HAPPEN IF YOU DO NOT GO AHEAD?

COMPLETE EACH SECTION AND SCORE EACH (1 IS LOW/WEAK, 10 IS HIGH/STRONG)	SCORE
FACTS & KNOWLEDGE GAPS	
SALES TARGET COMMITTED TO	
BARRIERS	
TIME INVESTMENT - REAL AND LAPSED	
FINANCIAL INVESTMENT	
COMPETITORS - STRENGTH	
SIZE OF OPPORTUNITY	
SYNERGY WITH CURRENT BUSINESS	
OPPORTUNITY COST	
BUSINESS RISK	
TOTAL SCORE	

It is likely that this will expose some serious gaps in knowledge and understanding. However, this should simply trigger activity to fill the knowledge gaps. Typically, innovation projects fail when they are allowed proceed in the absence of sufficient knowledge and facts. So, pausing at this stage to ensure that there is an adequate basis of information is essential. Real competitive knowledge and a detailed understanding off their offerings and customer perception is also often lacking. So, this may trigger a need to undertake fundamental competitor or market research to ensure that the landscape is properly understood.

It may seem perverse to seek a commitment from a sales perspective at this stage of the process. However, there is little point in developing a new product and service if the organisation lacks commitment to selling it and does not recognise the opportunity to achieve significant revenue growth.

So, you will now have a description and a score for each idea on your shortlist. You would also have exposed gaps in knowledge and commitment which will need to be addressed immediately to improve some of those scores.

Now rank the projects based on your scorecard with the highest scored projects at the top. How many you selected to proceed to the next stage will obviously depend on the level of resource at your disposal, typically I would select the top 25% for further refinement.

6.

How do I refine ideas?

So now we have our "short short" list we need to understand the level of interest and desire in the market, our ability to deliver and scale, profitability, and the likelihood of success in the external environment.

To achieve this, the ideal is to set out a mini business model for each of the innovation ideas.

Business Model

The "Business Model" is the blueprint which defines how your idea would operate and make money. The best way to visualise this is to use the Business Model Canvas created by Alexander Osterwalder and Yves Pigneur. The canvas sets out the 9 key parts to the business model covering Customers, Offering, Infrastructure and Financial Viability. These are all linked together so if something changes in one part of the model it affects some or all the others. The full Business Model Canvas was explored in the first book in this series (The Business Leaders Essential Guide to Growth).

Map each idea on a Business Model Canvas to identify how it fits, changes, or enhances the existing business model. At this stage there may well be many gaps. However, that should just trigger further thinking on how those gaps should be resolved during the research and development process. This is covered in the third section of this book. Try and avoid getting into too much detail and keep the model as simple and clear as possible.

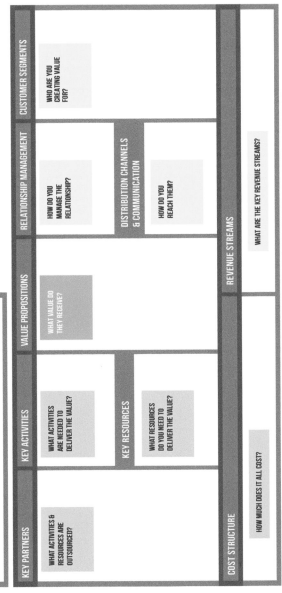

BUSINESS MODEL CANVAS

BUSINESS / PRODUCT DESCRIPTION

WHAT ARE WE FOCUSING ON?

KEY PARTNERS

WHAT ACTIVITIES & RESOURCES ARE OUTSOURCED?

KEY ACTIVITIES

WHAT ACTIVITIES ARE NEEDED TO DELIVER THE VALUE?

KEY RESOURCES

WHAT RESOURCES DO YOU NEED TO DELIVER THE VALUE?

VALUE PROPOSITIONS

WHAT VALUE DO THEY RECEIVE?

RELATIONSHIP MANAGEMENT

HOW DO YOU MANAGE THE RELATIONSHIP?

DISTRIBUTION CHANNELS & COMMUNICATION

HOW DO YOU REACH THEM?

CUSTOMER SEGMENTS

WHO ARE YOU CREATING VALUE FOR?

COST STRUCTURE

HOW MUCH DOES IT ALL COST?

REVENUE STREAMS

WHAT ARE THE KEY REVENUE STREAMS?

REF: "BUSINESS MODEL GENERATION" BY OSTERWALDER & PIGNEUR

Value Proposition

It is important to always keep the customer in mind when developing new initiatives and ideas. Therefore, having clarity on the value proposition at the earliest stage possible will help ensure that the project does deliver true value to the customer.

Customers are not interested in your products or solutions, they are primarily interested in their own problems, challenges, and desires. The value proposition must align with their agenda, which may also change through time, events, and experience.

Every business is based on satisfying customer needs and requirements by creating products and services which overcome their points of pain and create gains.

The Value Proposition provides a unifying focus by defining the:

- Value delivered
- Problem solved
- Product / Service offered
- Needs or wants satisfied

The full Value Proposition Canvas was explored in the second book in this series (The Business Leaders Essential Guide to Marketing).

(Tip: The best way to visualise this is to use the Value Proposition Canvas created by Alexander Osterwalder and Yves Pigneur.)

Map each project onto the Value Proposition Canvas to ensure that the problem solved, and the value delivered is clearly defined. This will then act as a reference point throughout the development process - are we still solving the problem? Are we still delivering the value?

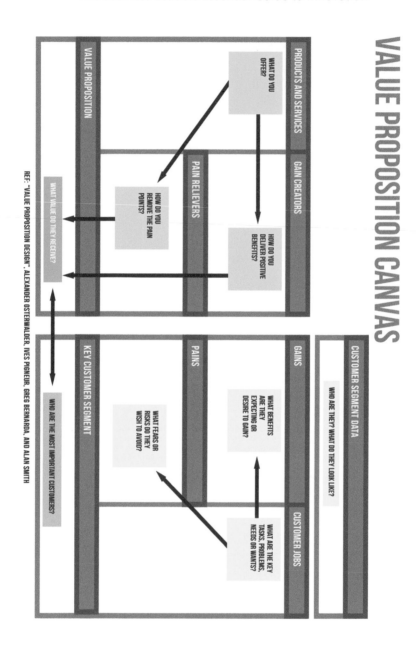

VALUE PROPOSITION CANVAS

VALUE PROPOSITION

PRODUCTS AND SERVICES
WHAT DO YOU OFFER?

GAIN CREATORS
HOW DO YOU DELIVER POSITIVE BENEFITS?

PAIN RELIEVERS
HOW DO YOU REMOVE THE PAIN POINTS?

WHAT VALUE DO THEY RECEIVE?

CUSTOMER SEGMENT DATA
WHO ARE THEY? WHAT DO THEY LOOK LIKE?

GAINS
WHAT BENEFITS ARE THEY EXPECTING OR DESIRE TO GAIN?

PAINS
WHAT FEARS OR RISKS DO THEY WISH TO AVOID?

CUSTOMER JOBS
WHAT ARE THE KEY TASKS, PROBLEMS, NEEDS OR WANTS?

KEY CUSTOMER SEGMENT
WHO ARE THE MOST IMPORTANT CUSTOMERS?

REF: "VALUE PROPOSITION DESIGN", ALEXANDER OSTERWALDER, IVES PIGNEUR, GREG BERNARDA, AND ALAN SMITH

The Greenhouse

Warning - Great ideas are killed off every day.

New ideas are extremely vulnerable in most organisations. The natural tendency is to kill anything new because it does not fit with the established way of thinking or the usual way of doing things - so we tend to reject them. Further, new ideas are only partly formed, clumsily articulated, riddled with inconsistencies, lacking detail, unproven and un researched - so are quite easy to knock down.

On top of this, "frazzled" executives already have overflowing "to do" lists and anything new is going to mean more work – so new ideas are seriously unwelcome.

New ideas and innovations often challenge existing profitable business activity, so organisations tend to delay for too long. Kodak invented the first digital camera but continued to be a "film" business until it was too late, and it was destroyed by its own invention.

The 9/11 attacks were predicted by two separate FBI agents - their ideas were rejected as hunches because they did not fit with existing thinking, and they could not prove them. Had these ideas been progressed or even just connected, history and many lives might have been different.

So new ideas need to be nurtured and developed ("green-housed") carefully - often best in a separate team away from the day-today maelstrom. Crazy ideas and hunches can change businesses radically, managing them properly can change the world.

7.

Who makes the final decision?

————⊃●○●⊂————

There should never be a single decision maker, with the power to approve or reject an innovation. No one person can have the full breadth of knowledge or skills to make that assessment. Instead, you should set up an "Innovation Board" with the remit of deciding which projects should be progressed, sent back for further thought or nurturing in the greenhouse or rejected. The board should aim to have a balanced range of projects from short, medium to long term.

Each idea should be presented to the Innovation Board supported by:

- Statement of Alignment
    - Aims, Goals and Objectives
    - Focus and Hit List
- Six Thinking Hats Summary
- Project Opportunity Scorecard
- Business Model
- Value Proposition
- Champion / Project Owner (Resource)

INNOVATION BOARD

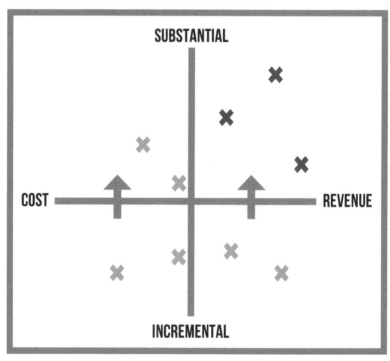

Assuming that multiple projects are approved for further development, it is essential that a summary of all projects is published using the Priority Plans process outlined in the first book in this series (The Business Leaders Essential Guide to Growth).

Priority "Breakthrough" Objectives (What)

Each of these objectives should begin with the word "To" and should be action orientated. They define "What" you want to achieve: To improve, to increase, to research, to launch, to develop etc. Each one should have a named "Champion" and a target completion date.

Priority Strategies (How)

Then for each of these objectives, list four key ways that they will be achieved.

This is the "How". Each of the "Hows" should have an individual named "Owner" and a target completion date. (Tip: Do not allow joint ownership, there needs to be clear responsibility)

So now you have priority objectives for your innovation projects each with several strategies defining how they will be achieved. Everything is owned and everything has a deadline.

PRIORITY PLANS

OVERALL GOAL	

PROJECT OBJECTIVES (WHAT)	PROJECT STRATEGIES (HOW) OR KEY STAGES - 'OWNER' :	DEADLINE:
PRIORITY 1 **CHAMPION:**	1 2 3 4	
PRIORITY 2 **CHAMPION:**	1 2 3 4	
PRIORITY 3 **CHAMPION:**	1 2 3 4	

8.

Who does what?

———◆◦◦◦◆———

Once approved by the innovation board, the innovation project can progress. However, to move into the development phase it will need to have a clear champion or owner and a team which brings together a wide range of skills, perspectives, attitudes, and personality types.

The skills required change significantly as the project progresses. In the ideation phase, creative skills will predominate, thereafter technical and engineering skills will come to the fore. Then detail, project management, scheduling, and reporting skills to ensure on-time implementation.

A project team with too many creative minds will simply keep on generating new ideas. A team with too many engineers will keep on developing and improving the product.

Team members should include those who have both the vision and the capability to turn the idea into innovation. There will need to be members with pragmatic and technical skills to ensure the development progresses and that setbacks are overcome. Team members who understand the customer perspective are essential, as are those who can harness internal communications to keep the wider business engaged. As the project moves closer to reality the team will need financial skills to help forecast the future impact.

This is the point at which the idea ceases to belong to the innovation team and demands input from the wider business.

HOW TO DEVELOP AND DELIVER INNOVATION

In this stage, the approved ideas are progressed, and project managed through initial customer feedback into development and delivery.

9.

How do I check that customers also like the idea?

———◦◦◦◦———

At the earliest opportunity validate the new development with a few customers. The idea may seem great to you but the sooner you know if customers might feel the same way the better. To have got to this stage you have already done a substantial amount of groundwork in understanding the type of customer, the problem solved, and the value delivered. So, get out and ask a few customers what their initial thoughts and reactions might be. The following questions provide a good basis for customer interviews to rapidly test the prototype or concept:

1. Recognition
(Do you recognise the customer situation, friction, problem, or opportunity?)

2. Clear
(Is the concept clear to you?)

3.Attractive
(Is the concept attractive to you?)

4. Fits the brand
(Does the concept fit with the brand?)

5. Buy
(How interested are you in buying the concept?)

6. Improvement
(How could the concept be improved?)

7. Barriers
(What would prevent you from buying this concept – other than cost?)

This early-stage customer feedback is akin to the "Chicken Test". When designing a new jet engine, there is one critical test it must pass – continuing to operate in the event of hitting a flock of birds. So rather than wait to the end of the lengthy and expensive development process, early-stage prototypes are set up and a whole dead chicken is thrown into the running engine. If the engine keeps running, it progresses to development. If not, much time and cost has been saved. So, it's always wise to "chicken test" the innovation project as soon as possible.

The danger of many innovation projects is that the teams become attached to them and therefore avoid early-stage testing. The harsh reality is, that if a customer does not "get it" when it is a new and exciting idea, then the chances are that they will not buy it months or years later. Of course, there are exceptions to this, which is why it is wise to have a balanced pipeline of innovations.

10.

How do I set up the development plan?

————⬦◉◉◉⬦————

Each of the projects should be defined at a high level with a named "champion" who oversees the project and reports back to the innovation board.

Priority Project Objective (What)

This sets out the key objectives for the project including specific outcomes and timeline. These should be challenging and aspirational as it is difficult to maintain energy and enthusiasm over extended periods.

Priority Project Development Stages (How)

The project is then broken down into its key stages with each stage allocated to an "owner" with a target completion date for each stage. Every element should have a single owner and a specific deadline. (Tip: Do not allow joint ownership, there needs to be clear responsibility)

So now each project has a clear objective and a range of strategies defining how they will be achieved. Everything is owned and has a deadline.

This then becomes the project development plan. This should be displayed publicly for everyone in the business to see. This way everyone knows who is leading which stage and can support or help. By keeping it visible it also applies some peer pressure to meet deadlines.

PRIORITY DEVELOPMENT PLANS

OVERALL PROJECT GOAL	

PROJECT KEY STAGES (WHAT)	PROJECT SUB STAGES - 'OWNER':	DEADLINE:
STAGE 1 CHAMPION:	1 2 3	
STAGE 2 CHAMPION:	1 2 3	
STAGE 3 CHAMPION:	1 2 3	

OKRs

One of the most visible ways of ensuring the whole busines understands the development plan is the OKR.

"OKRs have helped lead us to 10x growth, many times over. They have helped make our crazily bold mission of 'organizing the world's information' perhaps even achievable. They've kept me and the rest of the company on time and on track when it mattered the most" Larry Page, CEO of Alphabet and co-founder of Google.

Originally used at Intel, OKRs quickly became part of Google's culture as a management methodology to help ensure that the company focuses efforts on the same important issues throughout the organization.

OKRs comprise an **O**bjective (a clearly defined goal) and several **K**ey **R**esults (specific measures used to track the achievement of that goal).

The key result must be measurable, so at the end you can without any debate tell if it was done or not. No arguments, discussion, or judgements: Did I do that, or did I not do it? Yes? No?

The OKR Blueprint:

Objectives.
Define 3-5 key objectives on company, team, or personal levels.

Objectives should be Inspiring, Difficult, Explicit, Achievable.

They can be "Committed" or "Aspirational".

Key Results.
For each objective, define 3-5 measurable results.

Key results should be Specific, Measurable, Achievable, Relevant, Timebound, but not impossible.

OKR results could be based on growth, performance, revenue, or engagement.

Often, they are numerical, but they can also show if something is done or not done.

Publish & Share.
Ensure **all** OKRs are visible for **everyone** to see.
(Tip: its particularly important that the board of directors OKRs are visible)

OKR TEMPLATE

OVERALL PROJECT GOAL	WHAT DO YOU AIM TO ACHIEVE? WHAT IS THE GOAL?	
• IS IT INSPIRING, DIFFICULT, EXPLICIT, ACHIEVABLE? • IS IT COMMITTED (GUARANTEED) OR ASPIRATIONAL (STRETCHING? • IS IT PERSONAL, TEAM OR COMPANY GOAL?		
TO:		

KEY RESULTS	HOW WILL YOU DO THIS?	HOW WILL YOU KNOW YOU HAVE ACHIEVED IT?
• SPECIFIC, MEASURABLE, ACHIEVABLE, RELEVANT, TIMEBOUND "AS MEASURED BY..."		
1		
2		
3		
4		
5		

11.

How do I define action stages?

The project champion has already defined the key project objective and key stages. It is now necessary to set out detailed action stages, responsibility, dates, and measurement.

The level of detail required will depend on the complexity or length of the project, so be careful not to under simplify or over complicate.

One Page Plans

A simple One Page Plan format is ideal for this, created in a spreadsheet.

List the major stages or action steps to whatever level of detail is appropriate to the task. For each stage specify: **what** it is, **how** it will be done, **when** it will be done by (date), **who** will be doing it (responsibility), how you will know it has been completed (measurable), progress (status) and a column for comments.

The progress column should be categorised by status and colour:

Red   Off target, action required
Amber   In progress, not on target
Green   In progress, on target
White   Not started, scheduled later

The plan should be updated constantly by all project team members and published by a set time each week (e.g.14:00 every Friday).

This approach removes the need for update meetings to report on progress since that is self-evident from the document. It also means that the only items worthy of serious discussion are the red items which are off target and require action.

It always helps to get a plan down to a single page, as this significantly increases the likelihood of it being fulfilled.

How do I define action stages?

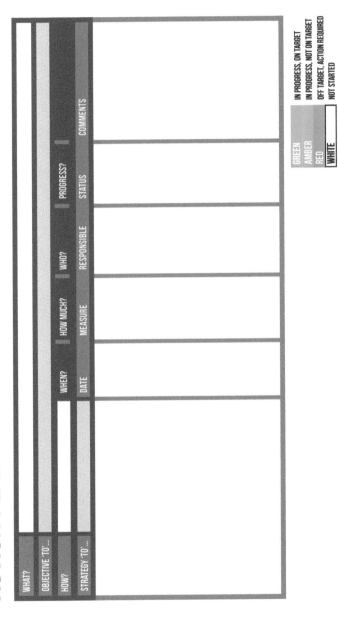

ACTION PLAN TEMPLATE

GREEN — IN PROGRESS, ON TARGET
AMBER — IN PROGRESS, NOT ON TARGET
RED — OFF TARGET, ACTION REQUIRED
WHITE — NOT STARTED

12.

How do I keep it on track?

———— ⋙⋘◆⋙⋘ ————

As the innovation project development progresses it is essential to keep on track of every single detailed action to ensure the project remains on target. The simplest way to achieve this is through a detailed weekly project list spreadsheet which is updated weekly by all team members, enabling project managers to review priorities and delays (changed target dates).

Every task item is entered with the name of its owner and a target completion date. Each week its status is updated with a brief progress update report, definition of the next action, and who owns that action. Any revisions in completion date are also logged. A summary report is then created which identifies the number of tasks in each stage of completion. High priority tasks should be highlighted in red, completed tasks in green. This way the overall project manager has complete visibility of every element of the project.

WEEKLY PROJECTS UPDATE

WC

WEEKLY PROJECTS LIST

LAST UPDATED:

KEY: RED = HIGH PRIORITY   GREEN = COMPLETED

PRIORITY	BUSINESS AREA	ITEM	STATUS	UPDATE REPORT	NEXT ACTION	BY WHO	DATE INITIATED	TARGET DATE	REVISED DATE	REVISED DATE	REVISED DATE	REVISED DATE	PROJECT OWNER

SUMMARY	STATUS	NO. PROJECTS
	LIVE	
	STALLED	
	ON HOLD	
	AWAITING BRIEF	
	NEW	
	COMPLETE	
	IN PROGRESS	

Project Management Plans

For more complex projects it is wise to undertake a more detailed project planning process. Use one of the many project management platforms to ensure that the project is broken down into appropriate stages, and that visibility is maintained on progress. These platforms also make it easier to manage projects with multiple partners in different locations without the need for lengthy time-wasting meetings.

The OOOO Model – how to make it happen

This framework tackles the issues of task ownership, clear objectives, focus on outcomes, and the need to be held to account:

Ownership

If no one owns it, it's no one's responsibility
if no one is responsible, no one cares
If no one cares, it's no one's priority
if it's no one's priority, it slips to the bottom of the To Do List
If it's at the bottom of the To Do List, it won't get done

Every part of the plan needs to have a single individual's name against it. Someone who owns it, is committed to it, feels responsible, and will feel recognised when they deliver. Never allow joint ownership of a strategy or task – joint ownership guarantees inefficiency and risks the critical task falling into the gap between the joint owners. Don't neglect to ensure that these tasks are included in appraisals and personal objectives. Your team needs to know this is serious not an optional add on task.

Objectives

Knowing what you are aiming at is essential to enable the team to focus and keep the purpose in mind. Clearly defined goals provide a reference point which enables everyone to filter out activities which do not align to the goal. This should also empower everyone in the team to question any activity which does not move the project forward. It is not unusual for the business owner to also be the most disruptive force. So, empowering your team to hold you to account also can be beneficial (if uncomfortable). Entrepreneurs have a habit of constantly thinking of new ideas, which they share with their team. The same team that is still wrestling to implement yesterday's great idea. So, yesterday's idea never gets finished and the team is confused, unproductive and demotivated. (Tip: keep a log of new ideas, reflect on them before sharing and have a category called "Next Year".)

Objectives should clearly define what is going to be different at the target date. This should be expanded so that the future state is more than a number, with some qualitative elements too. Do not forget the personal goals for the team and how this project will help achieve their aspirations too.

Outcomes

Whilst the overall objective is the goal, each stage in the plan will have its own outcomes which feed into other stages. Delay in any one stage will impact on subsequent stages. Therefore, the plan must have many defined results and milestones. This way you can be sure it stays on track, and you can take early corrective action if any stage stalls. What is measured gets done, so it is essential that everyone commits to the outcomes to be achieved. As always publish them and make them visible for all to see. If you are using the traffic light system outlined above, a weekly update on the whiteboard of how many tasks are Red, Amber or Green can provide a very simple visual prompt for all to see. Alternatively, you can establish more complex stages showing tasks which are Live, Stalled, On Hold, Awaiting Brief, New, Complete, In Progress etc.

Ouch

Ultimately every member of your team including yourself needs to be held to account to ensure key deadlines are met and that the desired pace of progress is achieved. If you are a business owner, you are your own boss, so it's down to you to hold yourself to account - or to give your team permission to do so. So, we need some pressure and may be a bit of pain to make things happen.

OOOO MODEL

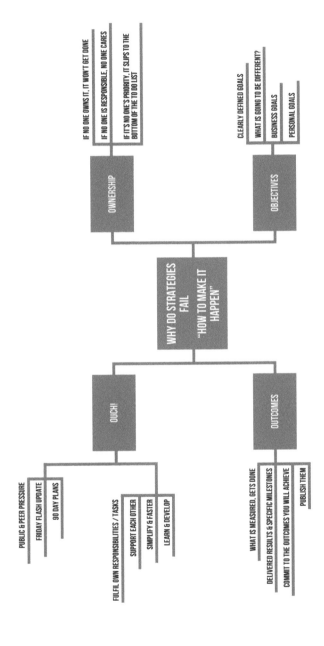

WHY DO STRATEGIES FAIL "HOW TO MAKE IT HAPPEN"

OWNERSHIP
- IF NO ONE OWNS IT, IT WON'T GET DONE
- IF NO ONE IS RESPONSIBLE, NO ONE CARES
- IF IT'S NO ONE'S PRIORITY, IT SLIPS TO THE BOTTOM OF THE TO DO LIST

OBJECTIVES
- CLEARLY DEFINED GOALS
- WHAT IS GOING TO BE DIFFERENT?
- BUSINESS GOALS
- PERSONAL GOALS

OUCH!
- PUBLIC & PEER PRESSURE
- FRIDAY FLASH UPDATE
- 90 DAY PLANS
- FULFIL OWN RESPONSIBILITIES / TASKS
- SUPPORT EACH OTHER
- SIMPLIFY & FASTER
- LEARN & DEVELOP

OUTCOMES
- WHAT IS MEASURED, GETS DONE
- DELIVERED RESULTS & SPECIFIC MILESTONES
- COMMIT TO THE OUTCOMES YOU WILL ACHIEVE
- PUBLISH THEM

Is this the end of the journey?
Not at all, you have still got all those ideas created and not progressed to go back to for further inspiration. Innovation is a constant and ongoing process, not a one-off event.

13.

What is going to get in your way?

Business as Usual

To achieve a significant change in performance a business needs to break out from "business as usual" – step change cannot be achieved by continuing in the same way but just working harder, it can only be achieved by working and thinking differently.

"The electric light did not come from the continuous improvement of candles." Oren Harari

Aiming too low

"The greatest danger for most of us is not that our aim is too high, and we miss it, but that it is too low, and we reach it." Michelangelo

Resistance
"To resist change is like holding your breath - if you persist, you die." Lao Tzu

Internal focus
"When the rate of change outside exceeds the rate of change inside, the end is in sight!" Jack Welch

Being reasonable and accepting the status quo
"The reasonable man adapts himself to the world. The unreasonable man insists that the world adapts to him. Therefore, all progress depends on the unreasonable man." George Bernard Shaw

"If we all worked on the assumption that what is accepted as true is really true, there would be little hope of advance." Orville Wright

Just being creative
"Creativity is thinking up new things. Innovation is doing new things." Theodore Levitt

"An idea that is developed and put into action is more important than an idea that exists only as an idea." Edward De Bono

Ignoring competitors
"Somewhere out there is a bullet with your company's name on it. Somewhere out there is a competitor, unborn and unknown, that will render your strategy obsolete. You can't dodge the bullet – you're going to have to shoot first. You're going to have to out-innovate the innovators." Gary Hamel

Incorrect expectations
"Most people overestimate what they can do in 1 year and underestimate what they can do in 10 years." Bill Gates

Inertia
"The system will always be defended by those countless people who have enough intellect to defend but not quite enough to innovate." Edward De Bono

"Change is the law of life. And those who look only to the past or present are certain to miss the future." John F. Kennedy

Ego
"A discussion should be a genuine attempt to explore a subject rather than a battle between competing egos. If you never change your mind, why have one?" Edward de Bono

Old ideas
"The problem is never how to get new innovative thoughts into your mind but how to get old ones out. Every mind is a building filled with archaic furniture. Clean out a corner of your mind and creativity will instantly fill it." Dee Hock

Getting lost in the detail
"You can't solve a problem on the same level it was created. You have to rise above it to the next level" Albert Einstein

14.

Recommended Reading

The Business Leaders Essential Guide to Growth
Stephen Dann

The Business Leaders Essential Guide to Marketing
Stephen Dann

The Invincible Company
Alexander Osterwalder, Ives Pigneur, Fred Etiemble and Alan Smith

Business Model Generation
Alexander Osterwalder and Ives Pigneur

Value Proposition Design
Alexander Osterwalder, Ives Pigneur, Greg Bernarda, and Alan Smith

The Design Thinking Playbook
Michael Lewrick, Patrick Link and Larry Leifer

Testing Business Ideas
David Bland and Alex Osterwalder

The Innovation Expedition
Gijs Van Wulfen

Where Good Ideas Come From
Steven Johnson

Lateral Thinking
Edward de Bono

Six Thinking Hats
Edward de Bono

How to Have Creative Ideas
Edward de Bono

The 5-day course in Thinking
Edward de Bono

Development Impact & You
Nesta

Factfulness
Hans, Ola & Anna Rosling

About the Author

$\Longrightarrow\!$

Stephen Dann is a creative thinker, innovator, marketer, strategist, author, and renowned business adviser.

He has built and led marketing teams in 5 major organisations building high performing teams, harnessing new technology and innovative approaches. Leaving corporate life behind, he developed a series of small and medium sized enterprises and fully experienced the highs and lows of the entrepreneurial journey.

He founded Business Impact Solutions Ltd in 2005 specifically to help business leaders and entrepreneurs tackle the challenges of growth, marketing, and innovation. As a business, management, and marketing consultant he has worked with over 400 client companies to date, ranging from mature global corporates and not for profit organisations to SMEs and high growth early-stage businesses across a wide range of sectors. He is a registered expert for the European Commission and is regularly called on to advise on the commercialisation of ground-breaking innovation.

Stephen is passionate about innovation, creativity, and change. He is recognised for seeking new ideas and insights to help businesses solve their commercial problems through creative and imaginative use of technology and marketing.

He believes that organisations only truly fulfil their potential and achieve their goals if they change the way they behave, change the way they operate or change some other fundamental aspect of the business. He constantly reminds business leaders that doing what you have always done and just exhorting teams to work harder is the best way to ensure those goals are not achieved.

Stephen is dedicated to helping businesses fix the problems that prevent organisations, teams, and individuals from achieving their potential.

As a sought-after business coach, consultant, and speaker, Stephen openly shares his tried, tested, and innovative approaches with entrepreneurs, business leaders and their teams.

Information on Stephen's books, insights and other materials can be found at:

www.businessimpactsolutions.co.uk

Lightning Source UK Ltd.
Milton Keynes UK
UKHW020719150522
403018UK00001B/2